OUR RESTLESS EARTH

OUR
RESTLESS EARTH

ROY A. GALLANT

ILLUSTRATIONS BY
ANNE CANEVARI GREEN

A FIRST BOOK
FRANKLIN WATTS 1986
NEW YORK • LONDON
TORONTO • SYDNEY

FRONTIS: WEATHERING WEARS AWAY MOUNTAINS
AND CREATES LANDSCAPES THAT ARE FAR MORE
DAZZLING THAN THE IMAGINATION COULD EVER
INVENT. SHOWN IS TOADSTOOL PARK IN NEBRASKA.

Library of Congress Cataloging in Publication Data

Gallant, Roy A.
Our restless earth.

(A First book)
Includes index.
Summary: Discusses the evidence gathered over the
years by geologists that has led them to formulate
certain theories about the formation of the earth and
the continual changes that have been taking place ever
since.
1. Geology—Juvenile literature.   (1. Geology)
I. Green, Anne Canevari, ill.   II. Title.
QE29.G35 1986   550   86-11176
ISBN 0-531-10205-X

FOR RUSTY

CONTENTS

ACKNOWLEDGMENTS

The author wishes to thank
Doubleday & Company and
Christopher J. Schuberth
for permission to adapt, for
inclusion in the present book,
certain short passages from
*Discovering Rocks
and Minerals*, by
Roy A. Gallant and
Christopher J. Schuberth,
copyright © 1967 by
Doubleday & Company.

My thanks also to
Dr. George Kukla, of
the Lamont-Doherty
Geological Observatory,
Palisades, New Jersey,
for his thoroughness in
reviewing the manuscript
of this book for accuracy.

CHAPTER ONE

A BEGINNING
FOR EARTH

The Solar System, which is our home, is an orderly community. It includes the Sun, which is an average-size star, and nine known planets along with their 60 or so moons. In addition, there are thousands of miniature planets, called asteroids, and billions of meteoroids and comets.

Modern astronomers think that the stars, along with their planets, formed out of huge cosmic clouds of gas and dust. Such clouds are called nebulae. We can see nebulae in many parts of our home galaxy, the Milky Way. We can also see them in galaxies far beyond our own.

The dust in the nebulae is made up of tiny bits of solid matter. The gas is mostly hydrogen. Hydrogen is the lightest and simplest of the more than 100 known chemical elements.

The Solar System was born about 4.6 billion years ago out of one such nebula cloud. The cloud stretched some 19 billion miles (30 billion km) across and contained about twice as much matter as the Sun has today. Gravity, which was strongest in the center of the cloud (where there was more gas and dust), pulled matter in from the outer thinner regions. Slowly the cloud collapsed in on itself. As it did, the matter in the center was packed together tighter and tighter and grew hot. The infall of matter also caused the cloud to start spinning and to spread out in a disk from around a central bulge. Eventually, about 90 percent of the cloud's gas and dust became part of a sphere forming at the center of the disk. After a time, this globe of hot matter began to glow a dull red. That is how astronomers think that our local star, the Sun, was born.

A great wheel of leftover material extended outward from the Sun's equator. Tiny dust grains within the disk were drawn together and began forming clumps. Clumps attracted other clumps. Many astronomers now think that just such a clumping process, called accretion, is what caused the planets and their moons to form. Some of the more solid clumps were made of various ices, others of rocky material, and still others of heavier matter, including iron and other metals. After about 100 million years, Earth probably had swept up about 98 percent of its present amount of matter.

At first, the young Sun was a relatively cool globe of gas that gradually drew large amounts of nearby disk material to itself. But farther out in the disk, near Jupiter, where the Sun's gravitational pull was weaker, larger amounts of disk matter remained. This may help explain why the inner planets (Mercury, Venus, Earth, and Mars) are small compared with the outer gas giant planets (Jupiter, Saturn, Uranus, and Neptune).

As the steady rain of matter continued down into the young Sun's core region, the core kept getting hotter. Soon the Sun heated up enough to glow a cherry red. Surrounding the young star was a dense fog of gas and dust containing the newly formed planets. Space throughout the Solar System at this time must have been extremely foggy.

After about 100 million years, the Sun became hot enough to shine with a yellowish-white light produced by nuclear fusion. (In nuclear fusion, the cores of atoms combine and so form a new element.) With its nuclear fires newly

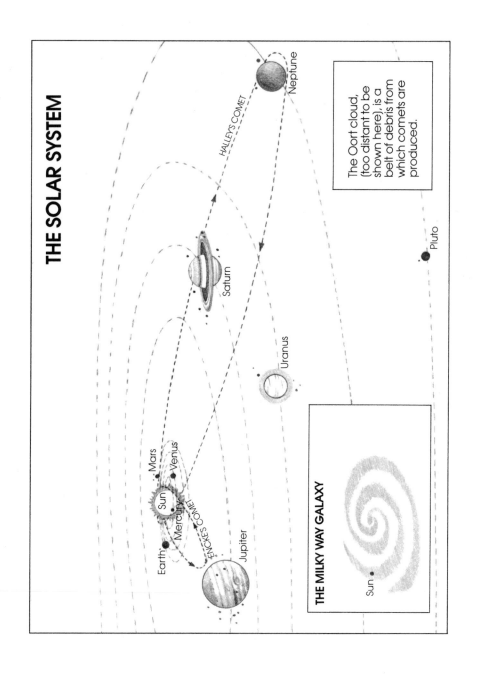

THE SOLAR SYSTEM

Neptune

HALLEY'S COMET

The Oort cloud, (too distant to be shown here), is a belt of debris from which comets are produced.

Saturn

Pluto

Uranus

Mars

Venus

Sun

Mercury

ENCKE'S COMET

Earth

Jupiter

THE MILKY WAY GALAXY

Sun

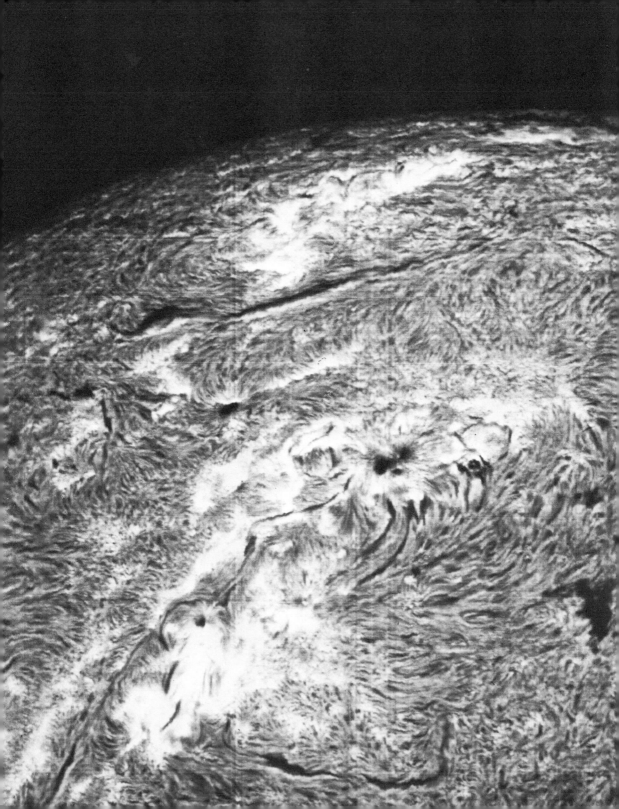

ignited, the Sun gave off huge bursts of energy that swept throughout the Solar System. These solar gales gradually cleared away the foggy gas and dust remaining in the disk. As this cosmic fog was blown away, space between the planets became clear, as it is today.

At the far outer edges of the Solar System a gigantic shell remained, made up of clumps of ice mixed with dust. This cloud of matter, called the Oort cloud, is believed to be the storehouse of comets. From time to time the gravity of a passing star flings one or more comets on a long inward journey that takes them around the Sun. Also, from time to time, some of the billions of asteroids smash into each other and break apart. Asteroids are lumps of rock and metal orbiting between Mars and Jupiter. They range in size from that of golf balls to mountain-size masses. Some of the broken pieces are flung far and wide and streak down through our atmosphere as meteors.

Although no one can say for certain that the Sun and its family of planets formed just this way, the evidence points to some such process. In any case, it seems almost certain that planets form right along with stars, and that stars are born out of the nebulae of space.

The seething surface of the Sun.

CHAPTER TWO

EARTH GETS A SOLID CRUST

THE HEATING UP OF EARTH

As Earth was forming out of the disk matter surrounding the new Sun, it began to heat up. Some of this heating was caused by clumps of matter, called planetesimals, in the solar disk. Some of the planetesimals were made of rock; others were made of rock mixed with iron and other metals.

As billions upon billions of planetesimals plunged into Earth during our planet's first 700 million years, they produced heat. The effect was the same as beating at the young Earth with a cosmic hammer.

Still more heat came from certain heavy atoms breaking apart. As they broke down, they released energy. This process is called radioactivity and goes on to this day within Earth.

At one point, Earth grew so hot that it glowed red as a soupy ball of melted rock and metals at a temperature of more than 3,600 degrees F (2,000 degrees C). Eventually, the heavy rain of planetesimals slowed as more and more of them were swept up by Earth and its neighboring planets. This allowed the soupy rock at the surface to cool and become solid in places. However, from time to time asteroid-size planetesimals smashed into the solid crust. This probably

Craters of the Moon are evidence that asteroids continued to plunge into Earth until only a few billion years ago.

kept the crust broken into rafts of solid rock floating in a sea of molten rock.

While the molten rock and metal materials floated about, the heavier matter sank into the central, or core, region. Such materials included the heavy metals iron and nickel. At the same time, lighter matter floated up to the surface. Such materials were mostly lightweight rock such as we find at the surface today.

As the crust continued to cool and form about 4 billion years ago, there were still many asteroid-size planetesimals orbiting in the regions of Mercury, Venus, Earth, and Mars. The many craters on the Moon and on these other planets are evidence that large numbers of asteroids continued to plunge into Earth until only a few billion years ago. Some scarred its surface, while other especially massive ones may have broken through the solid rock crust. As they did, huge amounts of molten rock welled up and spilled out over large areas. Evidence for a long rain of rock and metal planetesimals includes the large amounts of iron and other metals found mixed in with Earth's crustal rock. Because the crust was no longer molten when these late-arriving planetesimals struck the surface, the heavy metals in them remained part of Earth's crust instead of sinking into the iron and nickel core region.

Today, Earth is like a set of nesting globes. An eggshell-thin crust of solid rock is about 6 miles (9.6 km) thick beneath the oceans to about 37 miles (60 km) thick beneath the continents. Most of the continents are made up of a granite-type rock. Temperatures within the crust may range up to about 1,800 degrees F (980 degrees C). Beneath the crust is a much deeper layer called the mantle, which goes down to about 1,800 miles (2,900 km).

The mantle is made up of rock that contains a lot of iron and magnesium. Because the mantle rock is under more pressure than the crustal rock, it is hotter. Its matter may be squeezed this way and that, like toothpaste in its uncapped

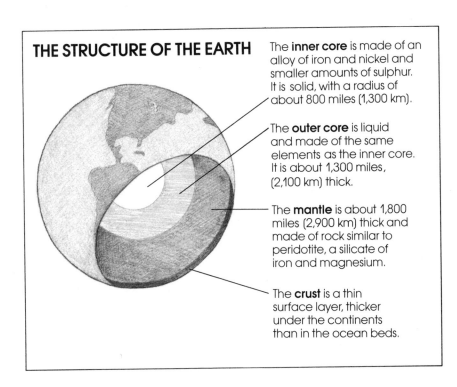

THE STRUCTURE OF THE EARTH

The **inner core** is made of an alloy of iron and nickel and smaller amounts of sulphur. It is solid, with a radius of about 800 miles (1,300 km).

The **outer core** is liquid and made of the same elements as the inner core. It is about 1,300 miles, (2,100 km) thick.

The **mantle** is about 1,800 miles (2,900 km) thick and made of rock similar to peridotite, a silicate of iron and magnesium.

The **crust** is a thin surface layer, thicker under the continents than in the ocean beds.

tube. The temperature of the mantle may range from about 950 degrees F (500 degrees C) to 7,500 degrees F (4,150 degrees C). The core seems to be a large ball of solid iron and nickel surrounded by a layer of liquid iron and nickel. It goes from a depth of about 1,800 miles (2,900 km) to 3,950 miles (6,360 km), which marks Earth's center. The temperature here may be about 7,000 degrees F (4,000 degrees C).

FORMATION OF
THE ATMOSPHERE

Exactly what Earth's first atmosphere was like is not known. But it was unlike the air we breathe today in that it had very little oxygen. Oxygen was not to be added to the air until about 4 billion years ago, as you will learn later.

During the planet's molten stage, many gases bubbled up out of the soupy rock and collected above the new planet as a primitive atmosphere. Among such gases there must have been large amounts of hydrogen, water vapor, nitrogen, carbon monoxide, and carbon dioxide. There may also have been smaller amounts of methane, which is a swamp gas, along with ammonia. Energy from the Sun would have broken up the water vapor into free oxygen and hydrogen. Because hydrogen is so light, it would have escaped Earth's gravitational grip, but the heavier oxygen would have stayed. The oxygen would then have combined with methane and changed it into carbon dioxide and more water vapor.

Meanwhile, heat beneath the crustal rock would have been causing other chemical reactions and sending great eruptions of more gases and hot lava boiling up to the surface as volcanoes. Over millions of years our hot planet would have belched forth huge amounts of steam, water, carbon dioxide, carbon monoxide, and nitrogen. The nitrogen that makes up most of our atmosphere today may have come from those millions of years of volcanic eruptions.

Earth's air probably did not get its rich supply of oxygen for millions of years more, not until there were green plants. The oxygen we breathe today is made by green plants. We could not survive without trees, bushes, grass, and other green plants.

THE FIRST OCEANS

Today, oceans cover almost three-quarters of Earth's surface. But that has not always been so. Some four billion years ago, Earth's crustal rock was still hot, and volcanoes were pouring out large amounts of water vapor and other gases.

As the water vapor rose into the cold upper atmosphere, it cooled, changed into liquid water, and fell to the surface as rain. But most of the rocky surface was not yet cool enough for the rain to settle and stay. As torrents of water poured down on the hot rock crust, the water instantly hissed skyward as clouds of steam.

Storm clouds must have blanketed our planet for millions of years, just as Venus's clouds blanket that planet today. Sunlight could not reach Earth's surface. But gradually the surface rocks cooled, and the rain was able to collect in pools. Streams, and then rivers, washed over the planet. They caused the rocks to cool more rapidly and cut ravines and canyons as the water flowed to the lowest levels.

For tens of millions of years the rains kept falling and flowing into basins that became the first seas. As the rivers and streams washed over the land, they picked up, dissolved, and carried salts with them. When the surface water of the oceans evaporated and fell back again as rain, the salts remained behind. In that way they collected in the seas, as they are still collecting today.

Eventually, after how many dark centuries we do not know, the great rains stopped. Dim light began shining through the thinning clouds, and one day the Sun's rays broke through, lighting a planet of jagged rock and sparkling blue water.

CHAPTER THREE

HOW ROCKS ARE MADE

Rocks are all around us—in the walls of rushing streams, along cliff faces, on mountainsides. They are everywhere.

To our eyes, the rocks of Earth's crust seem ageless, yet they are always changing. Forces within Earth squeeze the rock masses together and thrust them up as new mountain ranges. Slowly the mountains are worn away by ice, wind, and water, which carry bits and pieces of rock onto the land below, or out to sea. Called sediments, the bits and pieces pile up and form layer upon layer—as spreading fans along the foothills of mountains, or on the shallow seafloor near the shore. Century after century the loose sediments pile up, all the while being squeezed by the great weight of new sediments above. This squeezing process, combined with the great heat coming from below, causes the sediments to harden into rock.

Just as the sediments are turned into rock, the rock, in turn, may be changed by forces within Earth's crust. It may be melted, twisted, or folded, and gradually changed into a different kind of rock. This new rock may then be pushed up as a new mountain range, and then the process of wearing away begins anew.

*Gravel fans rise from the foothills of
the Panamint Range in California.*

IGNEOUS ROCK

If you were asked if you had ever watched a rock being formed, you probably would answer no. But you might be wrong. If you have ever seen liquid rock—called magma—flowing out of a volcano and spilling over the surrounding ground, you have seen igneous rock being made. The word *igneous* comes from the Latin word *igneus*, meaning "fiery." Magma that flows out of volcanoes and later hardens on Earth's surface is called lava. Magma seems to exist in great pockets of the solid crust, and probably within the mantle below the crust.

Magma often seeps its way up through a crack in the crust. Very often a large amount of magma hardens *before* it reaches the surface and forms a solid mass of igneous rock called a batholith. Batholiths may be hundreds of miles long and tens of miles wide.

Sometimes the magma forms a dome-shaped mass called a laccolith. Vertical or nearly vertical cracks that may be many miles long and contain hardened lava are called dikes. Magma that forces its way in between parallel layers of other rock and hardens forms a sill.

Batholiths, laccoliths, dikes, and sills form far below Earth's surface. Because they do, they are said to be intrusive igneous rock. This means that the magma has "intruded" into other rock, either by forcing an opening for itself or by melting its way through.

Since we cannot see intrusive igneous rock forming, how do we know about it?

Dried lava from an earlier eruption of the Kilauea Volcano in Hawaii; it had dried while flowing over a sea cliff.

Over the centuries, rain, wind, and ice wear away the surface rocks and gradually expose the ancient intrusive igneous rock. Such is the case of the Sierra Nevada Mountains and the famous sill of igneous rock called the Palisades that lies exposed along the Hudson River in New Jersey, opposite New York City. This sill formed about 190 million years ago.

Lava deposits are called extrusive igneous rock. All igneous rock, then, is either intrusive or extrusive, depending on where it hardens.

Intrusive and extrusive igneous rock also differ in the size of the mineral grains that form when the magma hardens. Most rocks are made of minerals. A mineral is any solid non-living element or compound found free in nature. Quartz, salt, and calcite are examples of minerals. Magma usually cools and hardens very slowly because it is insulated by surrounding rock. This slow cooling produces large mineral grains. Granite is an example of an intrusive igneous rock.

Lava cools and hardens quickly because of its sudden exposure to the cool air. This fast cooling results in the formation of very small mineral grains, such as those found in the common extrusive igneous rock basalt. Sometimes the cooling is so rapid that mineral grains do not form at all. This is the case with the volcanic glass obsidian.

SEDIMENTARY ROCK

About three-quarters of all the rocks we see at Earth's surface are sedimentary rocks. But if we drilled about halfway

Above: *a large dike in Huerfano County, Colorado.* Below: *a sill in the Taylor Glacier region of Antarctica*

A portion of the Palisades sill as it lies exposed
along the Hudson River in New Jersey

Quartz crystals, granite rock,
and the glass obsidian

down into Earth's crust, only about 5 percent of the rock would be sedimentary. Sedimentary rocks are made of bits and pieces of other kinds of rock, and they often contain fossils—the remains of once-living things. Blackboard chalk is sedimentary rock made of microscopic shells of sea animals that died and drifted to the ocean bottom millions of years ago.

Every time you walk through the sand at a beach, or step into the ooze of a lake bottom or over the pebbles, gravel, or clay of a streambed, you are walking on materials that millions of years from now may turn into sedimentary rock. Mud, lime, sand, and clay, as soft as they may be to touch, were once part of solid rock.

The rocks of mountains are cracked by frost and worn away by wind and water in a process called weathering. Small pieces of rocks are continually being broken off and carried away by mountain streams or rivers flowing toward the sea.

Certain rocky sections of the streambed or river may themselves be worn away by water. Or, as a river scours its bed and erodes its banks, materials such as mud and clay are swept along toward the sea. All of these bits and pieces of materials are sediments.

Sediments build up in layers. For example, for centuries a river may carry fine particles of clay down to the sea. Gradually the clay particles settle to the bottom of a bay. Then the river may speed up its flow and so begin to carry much heavier particles, such as sand. In this way, particles of sand are laid down on top of the clay. The bay may also go through a period of rich marine life. Over many years the

Fossils in limestone,
a sedimentary rock

The layering of sediments is obvious in this breathtaking landscape. Facing page: The rocks of mountains are cracked and worn by weathering.

marine creatures die, and their remains settle to the bottom and form a third layer of sediment. And so the process goes on.

You can see sediment layering when you examine sedimentary rocks along a cliff face. Each layer may be slightly different in color from the one above and below. Anyone who has seen the famous Painted Desert in Arizona can appreciate the wide color range of sedimentary rocks.

How do the soft sediments turn into hard rock? The gravels on a river bottom, or the fine sands on the ocean floor, are made up of billions of individual particles. Over time this soupy mass of particles may be cemented together by minerals, such as quartz and calcite, which act as a glue. If the sediments are made up of sand, the rock formed is sandstone. If the sediments are made up of gravel, the sedimentary rock is called conglomerate. This process of making sedimentary rocks is called cementation.

METAMORPHIC ROCK

As you learned earlier, deep within Earth's crust—6 miles (9.6 km) or so—the rock is under great pressure and is very hot. It is here that we find igneous and sedimentary rock being changed into the third major rock type—metamorphic rock. Metamorphic means ''change of form.''

The heat and pressure deep within Earth's crust are so great that the rock there is not solid in the same way that rocks on Earth's surface are solid. Like soft putty, rock deep within the crust can be bent, folded, squeezed, and stretched into any shape.

The great pressures and high temperatures within Earth's crust that crumple rock as though it were paper change the very substance of the original rock. The old minerals are changed into new ones. These new mineral grains are large

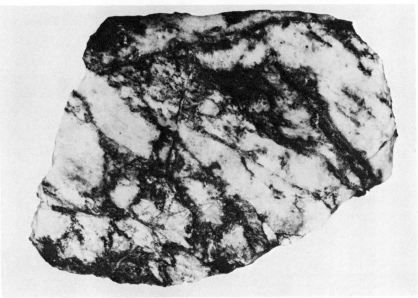

Slate (above) and marble

ROCKS FORMED BY HEAT
(IGNEOUS ROCK)

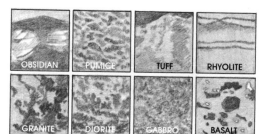

OBSIDIAN | PUMICE | TUFF | RHYOLITE

GRANITE | DIORITE | GABBRO | BASALT

ROCKS FORMED BY PRESSURE
(SEDIMENTARY ROCK)

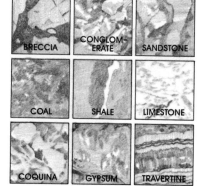

BRECCIA | CONGLOM-ERATE | SANDSTONE

COAL | SHALE | LIMESTONE

COQUINA | GYPSUM | TRAVERTINE

ROCKS THAT CHANGE
(METAMORPHIC ROCK)

Limestone becomes marble, sandstone turns to quartzite, and shale becomes slate, then schist, then gneiss, and finally granite.

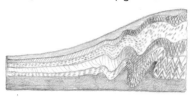

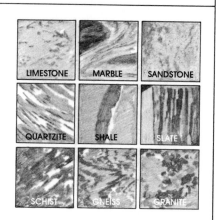

LIMESTONE | MARBLE | SANDSTONE

QUARTZITE | SHALE | SLATE

SCHIST | GNEISS | GRANITE

enough to see without a magnifying glass. Sometimes they are flat and arranged in stacks, as in the case of mica.

Metamorphic rock can also be formed when magma deep within the crust melts its way through surrounding rock and forms batholiths, dikes, and sills. Where the hot magma comes in contact with the surrounding solid rock, metamorphic rock is formed. Batholiths form thick belts of metamorphic rock, sometimes a few hundred feet wide. Thin dikes or sills often form bands only a few feet wide. It is in these zones that some of the most interesting minerals can be found. Ore mines also are often located in such zones.

In the first kind of metamorphic rock formation, heat and pressure act together to produce new rock. Slate is formed that way. In the second kind, heat is the main cause. Marble is a common rock produced mainly by heat.

Of the three kinds of rock described in this chapter, igneous rocks make up most of Earth's crust, about 65 percent. Metamorphic rocks are next, at 27 percent. And sedimentary rocks make up about 8 percent of the crust. The most plentiful minerals are quartz and feldspar, making up 63 percent of the crustal rock.

How do scientists use their knowledge of rock types and rock formations to read the rock record and learn about Earth's long history? We'll look at that next.

CHAPTER FOUR

READING THE
ROCK RECORD

HOW FOSSILS ARE USED

Our knowledge of animals and plants that lived millions of years ago comes mainly from fossils and the rocks in which we find them entombed. The fossil record suggests to us that all animals and plants living today had ancestors that lived on Earth long ago. Most groups of animals and plants that lived millions and hundreds of millions of years ago died out, or became extinct.

That's what happened to the once-mighty dinosaurs. Almost all we know about the dinosaurs and other extinct groups comes from a study of their fossil remains and the rocks that contain the fossils.

But fossils tell us a lot more about Earth's past than this. They also tell us much about the continents and seas of ancient times. When paleontologists, scientists who study fossils, find stumps of fossil trees in places now covered by water, they know that such places were once dry land. And when they find rocks containing ancient sea creatures, such as corals, trilobites, and brachiopods, they know that an ancient sea once covered the land where the fossils of those ocean-living animals now lie. Further, by following along the edge of that fossil-bearing rock, they can map the outline of that ancient sea.

Fossils also tell us many things about the climate of past ages. Suppose you found fossil tree ferns or fossil magnolia plants beneath the ice sheets of Antarctica or Greenland? Scientists have actually found such plants in both of those places. Like the scientists, you might conclude that the climate of Greenland and Antarctica was much warmer millions of years ago, and so it was.

Coal deposits usually contain the remains of tree ferns and other plants. These plants suggest a warm and swampy region when the coal deposits were being formed. But today, many such coal deposits are found in parts of the world that are cold and dry, again such as Antarctica. So the

Coal deposits often contain fossils or fossil imprints of tree ferns.

climate in such places had to be much different then from what it is today in order for warm swamplands to have existed there.

But we still have not talked about one of the most important uses of fossils. Fossils give us clues about the age of the rocks that contain them.

DATING EARTH'S ROCKS

Earlier we mentioned that sediments are laid down on the seafloor in layers. For years a river might carry mostly mud down to the sea. The mud is deposited on the floor of the bay at the mouth of the river and forms a thick carpet. Then the river changes and most of its sediments become silt rather than clay. A carpet of silt is now laid down on top of the clay. Still later, the main sediment carried by the river may be fine sand.

Suppose at this point that you push a hollow tube down into the floor of the bay and then pull it up. The tube would contain a neat layering of sediments: clay at the bottom, silt in the middle, and sand on top. Scientists call such a tube of sediments a core sample. If you did not know the history of the river, your core sample would tell you. In any normal layering of sediments, or rock, the more recent layers are found on top of older layers. This is called the law of superposition.

TOPSY-TURVY ROCK RECORDS

It is tempting to assume that the top layer in a many-layered column of rock is always the most recent and the bottom layer is the oldest. But things are not always that simple. Earth is an ever-changing planet, and its rock crust is restless, as rivers cut through the rock and new mountain ranges form. As mountains are thrust up, the rock layers become twisted.

Upturned sedimentary rock layers such as this one can confuse fossil dating.

Each rock layer has its own group of fossils,
which help scientists to properly date the layer.

They may be broken or bent so they appear edge up. They may even be turned completely upside down. Sometimes the paleontologist doesn't know if the most recent layer is on the top or bottom.

Fossils have helped solve this problem. By studying the fossil groups in a layer of sedimentary rock, scientists are able to say that one layer is more recent or older than a layer above or below. Each rock layer nearly always has its own special group of fossils.

For nearly 200 years, paleontologists all over the world have studied in what succession the fossils occur in rocks. Today, because they know that certain fossils are older or more recent than certain other fossils, they can use the fossils as a clue to the age of the rocks. So each kind of fossil has a special time period when the animal or plant lived. When scientists learned that fossils could help them date rock layers, they could begin to understand the long and tangled history of Earth.

CHAPTER FIVE

TELLING
GEOLOGIC TIME

The history of life on Earth goes back much longer than scientists of only a few years ago realized. We now know that simple plantlike organisms lived about 3.8 billion years ago. This means that life established itself on this planet less than one billion years after the Sun and planets were formed. One of the tasks of geologists and paleontologists has been to understand how living forms evolved over millions of years and come up with a fossil calendar.

Around the year 1800, an English engineer named William Smith learned that the success of different engineering projects—especially the building of canals—depended on the kind of rock found in the region where the canal was to be dug. As he studied different rock layers, he saw that many of them had fossils. Soon he noticed that any single rock layer usually contained the same assemblage of fossils. The younger rock layers above, and the older rock layers below, each had different kinds of fossils. Two French scientists, Georges Cuvier and Alexandre Brongniart, also noticed that certain rock layers contained unique assemblages of fossils. They made this observation while studying and mapping the fossil-bearing rock layers that surrounded Paris.

Cuvier discovered something else important about fossils. He compared all the fossils he had dug up around Paris with living animals known to him. He soon found that the fossils from the upper rock layers, which were the most recent layers, were more like the animals living today than were those fossils from the deeper rock layers, which were older.

The work of Smith, Cuvier, and others clearly showed that some fossils were older than others. But one question that troubled these men was exactly how old a given fossil was—ten thousand, ten million, or ten hundred million years?

Scientists came to learn that many events in Earth's long history must have occurred over vast expanses of time called geologic time. Geologic time does not tick off a century or two but millions of years in our planet's history.

Around 1900, scientists learned that radioactive elements decay (lose some of their subatomic particles) at certain rates and turn those elements into different ones. For instance, uranium changes into lead, and potassium changes into argon. This happens because the individual atoms in these elements are big and have many neutrons. The large number of neutrons makes the atom unstable, meaning that the atom loses some of its neutrons. It is this loss of neutrons that changes the element into a different element.

A scientist dating a rock sample, for instance, compares the number of unchanged uranium atoms with the number of atoms that have changed into lead. The amount of time needed for half the atoms of a radioactive element to change is called the element's half-life.

Nothing seems to affect the half-life of any radioactive element—not even changes in temperature or pressure. Since the scientist knows the half-life of the radioactive element, and since the number of new (lead) atoms can be compared to the number of old (uranium) atoms, it is a sim-

Meteorites are the oldest known objects in the Solar System, as far as we can tell. This is an iron meteorite found in central Australia.

ple matter then to tell how long the radioactive "clock" has been running.

Different radioactive elements have different half-lives. For example, uranium-238 changes to lead-206 in 4,510 million years.

It is because each radioactive element has its own private rate of decay that it can be used as an "atomic clock." Atomic clocks give scientists an accurate way to say that one rock is 170 million years old, for example, and that another is only 30 million years old. And any fossil group contained in the 170-million-year-old rock must also be around 170 million years old.

Knowing the age of such a fossil group, then, tells the scientist that any other type of rock containing fossils of that kind anywhere in the world must also be 170 million years old. With the discovery of atomic clocks, a new chapter in the story of telling geologic time was written. It meant that paleontologists could measure quite exactly when certain events occurred in Earth's very long history.

By using atomic clocks, scientists have found that meteorites are the oldest known objects in the Solar System whose age we can measure directly. Measurements generally show an age of 4.6 billion years for the formation of meteorites. And since meteorites almost certainly were formed right along with the planets, we accept that age for Earth as well.

Moon rocks brought back to Earth by the *Apollo* astronauts are also 4.6 billion years old. The oldest Earth rock measured so far is a volcanic boulder from West Greenland. Its computed age is 3.8 billion years. For the first 800 million years of Earth's history, the crust was too hot to be solid and form any solid rock.

CHAPTER SIX

GIANT RAFTS
OF STONE

One of the greatest leaps in our understanding of Earth was the discovery that its oceans and lands are ever changing. The fossil and geological evidence for such changes in land and sea point to a view of the continents as giant rafts of stone drifting about in a sea of hot, puttylike rock in which the continents are rooted.

Like great, slow-moving ships of stone, the continents have been drifting about ever since Earth developed a solid crust some 4 billion years ago.

A SUPERCONTINENT BREAKS UP

The continents may have begun as small blocks of cooling rock that bumped into each other and stuck together, then broke apart and rejoined again and again. In the hearts of the present-day continents geologists have found what they believe to be traces of the original blocks of rock.

By about 220 million years ago the early continents seem to have merged into a single supercontinent called Pangaea. That was during the geologic time period known as the Triassic, which marks the early years of the so-called Age of Reptiles. By about 135 million years ago, Pangaea had bro-

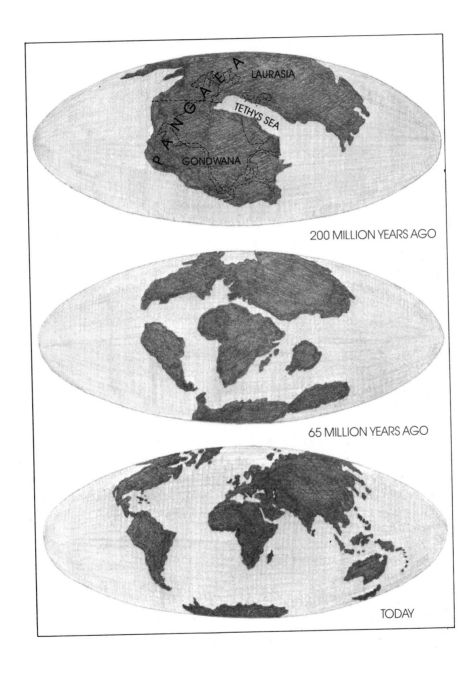

LAURASIA

PANGAEA

TETHYS SEA

GONDWANA

200 MILLION YEARS AGO

65 MILLION YEARS AGO

TODAY

ken up and drifted apart into a northern half called Laurasia and a southern half called Gondwana. This was during the Cretaceous period, by the end of which the last of the dinosaurs had become extinct. By 65 million years ago these two huge landmasses had split further, and the pieces had drifted toward the positions of the continents we know today.

CONTINENTAL DRIFT
AND CLIMATE CHANGE

From time to time in Earth's past, entire species of plants and animals have died out, or become extinct. There have also been periods of massive extinctions, when many thousands of species died out over relatively short periods of time in the geologic calendar. Drastic changes in climate—a period of warming and drying, a period of cooling, a period of drought—can cause species not used to the new climate conditions to die out.

The drifting about of the continents and mountain building are major causes of climate changes. As the enormous crustal rafts of the continents slide over the molten rock beneath and grind up against one another, they thrust up mountains in one place and leave enormous depressions in other places. This changes the shape and the height of the land and the shape and depth of the oceans. The result is a change in sea level and the way ocean currents flow. Those conditions in turn bring a change in the distribution of warm winds and rains.

The continents are made up mostly of material rich in alumina silicates, which are light in weight and color. Alumina silicates are a compound, a blend of the elements aluminum, silicon, and oxygen. Because granite is the most common rock of this type, the continents are usually described as granitic. The seafloor, on the other hand, is made up chiefly of rocks rich in silica and magnesium, material that is heavy and dark. Since basalt is the most common rock in this zone, the crust of the ocean floor is usually described as basaltic.

PLATE TECTONICS

The idea that the continents move about was first suggested by the fact that the edges of Africa and South America fit neatly together like pieces of a jigsaw puzzle. So do the edges of the United States and Europe. In 1912, the German weather scientist Alfred Wegener presented his arguments for wandering continents in a book. In addition to the jigsaw-puzzle fit, Wegener said that the rocks and fossils on opposite shores of the Atlantic Ocean were so alike that the two shores must have been joined in the distant past. He wrote: "It is just as if we were to refit the torn pieces of a newspaper . . . and then check whether the lines of print run smoothly across. If they do, there is nothing left but to conclude that the pieces were in fact joined in this way." Most scientists at the time laughed at Wegener's ideas.

Among the first bits of physical evidence for drifting continents was the discovery of many undersea mountain ridges. In the 1950s, Columbia University scientists Maurcie Ewing and Bruce C. Heezen showed that the ridges actually form a continuing chain of mountains that winds its way around the globe over a distance of 40,000 miles (64,000 km). In some places the ridge is hundreds of miles wide and rises more than a mile above the seafloor. Some of the higher peaks of the ridge poke above the ocean surface and form islands such as Easter Island and the Azores.

All along the top of the ridge is a trench called a rift valley. The trench marks a line along which molten rock from the mantle wells up, cools, and forms new crust. As it does, it causes the seafloor to spread out on both sides of the ridge. This means that the United States and Europe, for example,

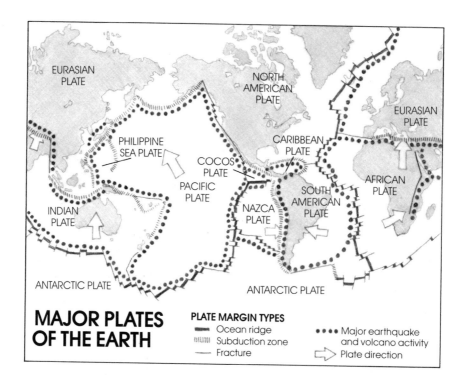

MAJOR PLATES OF THE EARTH

PLATE MARGIN TYPES
- Ocean ridge
- Subduction zone
- Fracture
- •••• Major earthquake and volcano activity
- Plate direction

are being pushed farther away from each other by about 1 inch (2.5 cm) a year.

More evidence for the wandering continents theory came from fossils. In the 1960s, fossil bones of a mammal-like reptile called *Lystrosaurus* were found in gravel deposits in Antarctica. The animal lived in warm swamps about 300 million years ago and became extinct during the Jurassic period. Before the 1960s, fossils of *Lystrosaurus* had been discovered in South Africa, India, and China. Their appearance in Antarctica surprised everyone. How could they have gotten there? There is no way the animal could have swum across the seas and reached Antarctica. Fossils of other animals, and of plants found in Antarctica that resemble fossils found in Africa and India, are further evidence that those continents were once joined and shared a common warm climate before they drifted apart.

The continents can wander about because they are made of lightweight rock floating in a puttylike sea of the dense upper mantle rock. They are moved about by the upwelling, churning, and explosive action of the upper mantle rock. Along with large sections of ocean floor, the continents are pushed about as giant rafts, called plates.

The theory of continental drift is also known as plate tectonics. There seem to be six major plates and about a dozen smaller ones. Sometimes the edges of two neighboring plates grind together. Such zones tend to have lots of earthquakes (marked by dots in diagram).

When two plates ram each other, something has to happen along their edges. For instance, seafloor spreading pushes the Nazca plate (see diagram) eastward against the American plate along the coasts of Chile and Peru in South America. Meanwhile, the American plate is being pushed westward, also by seafloor spreading along the Mid-Atlantic Ridge. The lighter continental rock of the American plate rides up over the heavier basaltic rock of the Nazca plate. The forward-moving edge of the Nazca plate is pushed down into the hot mantle rock under the edge of the American plate. The heat of the mantle rock then melts the leading edge of the Nazca plate. This newly melted rock next forces its way up through the American plate and from time to time flows to the surface as volcanoes.

This pushing and shoving of one plate against another produces mountain ranges such as the mighty Andes and zones of heavy earthquake activity. Where one major plate is pushed down beneath another, a deep ocean trench is formed. There are several such trenches in the Pacific Ocean, including the Aleutian Trench, the Japan Trench, and the Marianas Trench. All are about 6 miles (9.6 km) deep

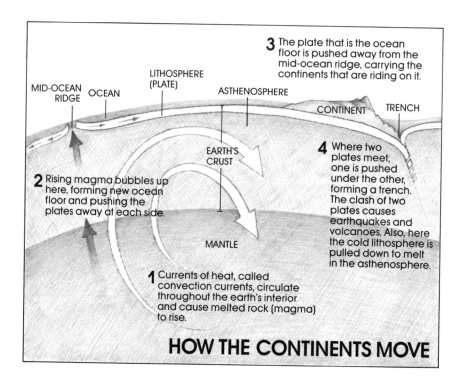

3 The plate that is the ocean floor is pushed away from the mid-ocean ridge, carrying the continents that are riding on it.

LITHOSPHERE (PLATE)

ASTHENOSPHERE

MID-OCEAN RIDGE OCEAN

CONTINENT   TRENCH

EARTH'S CRUST

2 Rising magma bubbles up here, forming new ocean floor and pushing the plates away at each side.

4 Where two plates meet, one is pushed under the other, forming a trench. The clash of two plates causes earthquakes and volcanoes. Also, here the cold lithosphere is pulled down to melt in the asthenosphere.

MANTLE

1 Currents of heat, called convection currents, circulate throughout the earth's interior and cause melted rock (magma) to rise.

HOW THE CONTINENTS MOVE

and are steep-walled on their land side and gently sloping on their ocean side. Sometimes when two plates collide, their edges blend into one another, and in the process land is pushed up. This seems to be the way the Himalayan Mountains and the Tibetan Plateau were formed.

Undersea mountains are produced by molten rock oozing up out of the hot upper mantle. In places there are hot spots in the ocean floor. Magma wells up through these chimney-like hot spots and slowly builds an undersea mountain. Eventually the mountain grows high enough to rise above the surface.

Meanwhile, the ocean-floor plate moves along and passes over the hot spot. Another mountain is then formed behind the first one. And then another and another until a chain of undersea mountains forms what geographers call an archipelago.

The Hawaiian Islands were made in this way. The youngest of the Hawaiian Islands, Hawaii, is the easternmost island in the group, with rocks only a million or two years old. The Midway group of islands are at the opposite end of the chain and are the oldest, some 25 million years old. We'll talk more about mountain building in a later chapter. First let's look more closely at the more sudden events that disrupt Earth's surface—earthquakes and volcanoes.

CHAPTER SEVEN

VOLCANOES AND EARTHQUAKES: CLUES TO EARTH'S INTERIOR

VOLCANOES

Volcanoes give us a direct way of examining the kinds and nature of the materials located beneath Earth's crust. In violent volcanic eruptions we can expect a certain sequence of events. First there are small, local earthquakes surrounding the volcanic mountain about to become active, as was the case with Mount St. Helens in 1980. These earthquakes may be accompanied by deep-throated rumblings. Sometimes a lake near the volcano suddenly disappears or changes its level. This happens just before the mountain erupts. Great blasts of steam roar out of the crater to heights of thousands of feet. During the 1779 eruption of Mount Vesuvius, in Italy, steam reportedly rose 2 miles (3.2 km) above the crater.

Mixed with the steam are gases, rocks, dust, and ashes, which are tossed and blown about this way and that. When the famous volcanic island of Krakatoa, near Java and Sumatra, blew its top in 1883, it erupted in a series of explosions. Then, on the following day, August 27, there was one mighty blast of flame, smoke, and ash that rose 17 miles (27.2 km) into the air. When the sea calmed and the air cleared, there was nothing left. The mountain was gone. The noise

The steam in volcanoes is mixed with gases, dust, rocks, and ashes. Shown is the great eruption that took place in May 1980 on Mt. St. Helens in the state of Washington.

from the explosion was heard 1,700 miles (2,720 km) away in Australia.

The steam rising out of an erupting volcano's crater condenses and falls back to the ground as rain. As it falls, it mixes with the dust and ashes and splatters to the ground in torrents of mud. Thunder and lightning boom and flash around the top of the mountain. Eventually, magma deep within the mountain wells up and floods over the crater walls, pouring down the mountainside in great glowing rivers of lava.

Meanwhile, blobs of flaming lava may be blasted out of the crater and hurled thousands of feet into the air. These volcanic bombs solidify and fall back to earth. Cotopaxi in Ecuador reportedly tossed a 200-ton block of stone 9 miles (14.4 km). No wonder people of old looked on active volcanoes as entrances to the lower world of fire. In fact, the word *volcano* comes from the Italian *vulcano*, so named in honor of the Roman god of fire, Vulcan. There are in the world today about 500 major active volcanoes, not including many yet undiscovered ones beneath the seas.

The gases released during an eruption are mostly water vapor and carbon dioxide; also included are sulfur dioxide, hydrogen chloride, and hydrogen. The gas cloud that puffs out of a volcano is more than 90 percent water vapor. Scientists are not sure just where all this water comes from.

As the gases escape, the magma becomes more fluid, welling up to the surface more rapidly. Sometimes a magma flow continues to eat its way through Earth's crustal rock for millions of years. Magma pours out of a volcano's feeding pipe as red-hot or white-hot lava at a temperature of about 2,000 degrees F (1,100 degrees C).

EARTHQUAKES

Like volcanoes, earthquakes have been common throughout Earth's history. Also, like volcanoes, earthquakes can be used to find out about the kinds and nature of the materials in the mantle rock beneath the continents, and down into Earth's very core.

Perhaps you have felt an earthquake shake the ground beneath your feet. One of the most destructive earthquakes in recorded history shook the Japanese cities of Yokohama and Tokyo on September 1, 1923.

In the areas affected by the earthquake and then gripped by fire, about 100,000 people were killed. An additional 100,000 were injured and about 43,000 were missing.

What causes earthquakes? The Japan earthquake of 1923 was caused by a movement along a great fault, or crack, in the bottom of Sagami Bay. A fault is nothing more than a break in the crustal rock. Year after year the two surfaces along a fault may press against each other without causing a disturbance. But eventually the pressure may become so great that the two surfaces slip, or snap. When the snapping takes place, violent vibrations shiver through the ground and may topple buildings for miles around. Thousands, if not millions, of faults thread their way across the globe, but just how deeply these great cracks extend into the crustal rock is still not known.

One of the most spectacular faults visible is the San Andreas fault in California. This fault is the dividing line between two great blocks of Earth's crust grinding against each other. The fault runs some 620 miles (1,000 km) across California's coastal mountain ranges.

Tens of thousands of earthquakes occur each year. Whenever one of them bumps, jars, or shakes us, it sends out waves from the region where the quake occurs (called the focus) to points all over the world. Some of these waves pass right through the planet; others travel around Earth along its curved surface.

Scientists can produce similar waves by setting off explosions of dynamite, for example. Then, by studying how the

waves behave, they can learn many things about the planet's interior.

When an earthquake snaps a fault, earthquake waves, called seismic waves, can be recorded on seismographs at seismograph stations all over the world. Basically, a seismograph is a pendulum with a pen hanging from it. Beneath the pen is a drum of paper that rotates day and night. When all is quiet the pen traces a straight line on the moving paper. However, when an earthquake shakes the seismograph station, the frame supporting the pendulum moves, but the pendulum does not. The result is an inked wiggly line, called a seismogram, that shows when the earthquake occurred and how severe it was. The more pronounced the wiggles, the more severe the earthquake.

The first group of seismic waves recorded by a seismograph are P ("primary") waves. They are the first to reach an earthquake station because they travel faster than the other waves. The second group of seismic waves to reach the station are called S ("secondary") waves. When P and S waves reach the surface, they set up a third class of waves called surface waves. The surface waves are the slowest of all and are the ones that cause damage during an earthquake.

One very useful thing scientists have learned about seismic waves is that the P waves can travel through solid rock, molten rock, or gases. But S waves can travel only through solids. Another useful bit of information about the waves is

The San Andreas Fault (horizontal line across center of picture). Note how the meandering streambed has been shifted as a result of activity around the fault.

that they travel faster through denser material such as iron than they do through less dense material such as granite.

With the knowledge that P and S waves travel at different speeds and behave differently in different kinds of materials, scientists have been able to learn about the makeup of Earth from its surface down to its very center. For example, they have found that the crust must be made up of rocky matter of different densities—lightweight rock and heavier rock, including granite, marble, shale, limestone, basalt, and others. This is the picture down to a depth of about 20 to 30 miles (32 to 48 km). Then the picture changes. Beneath the eggshell-thin crust is the rock of the mantle layer, probably containing iron and magnesium mixed in with silicates. Because the mantle rock is under very high pressure from the weight of the crust above, its upper rock acts like putty. But lower down, the mantle rock is rigid. Beneath the mantle layer is the core, made of still denser matter, with an outer liquid core probably made of iron and nickel and an inner solid core of the same material.

So the study of earthquake waves has given us this picture of Earth's interior. We walk on a thin solid-rock crust about 37 miles (59.2 km) deep. Below is hot mantle rock reaching to a depth of about 1,800 miles (2,880 km). And at the center is a core of solid iron and nickel wrapped in a coating of liquid iron and nickel at a depth of about 3,950 miles (6,320 km).

CHAPTER EIGHT

MOUNTAINS FROM DITCHES

Anyone who has gazed upon the Alps, Rockies, or other high peaks may have had the feeling that time stands still there. In the mountains, more than anywhere else, change seems the least noticeable. The mountains somehow seem permanent, indestructible, unchangeable. But they are not. As surely as the sea is ever changing the shorelines of the continents, wind, rain, and frost are sculpting the mountains ever so slowly in a continuous process of change. Meanwhile, new mountains are in the making.

In Earth's history there have been about ten major periods of crustal upheaval during which mountains have been upthrust. Some 225 million years ago the young Appalachians, now gentle and rounded with age, were splendid snowcapped peaks, possibly as mighty as the Alps. They ran from Newfoundland to Alabama. But century after century the forces of erosion have smoothed and leveled them. However, as old mountains like the Appalachians age and die, new ones are born.

We are now living in a period of mountain building. In fact, ever since people have roamed over this planet, mountains have been buckling up out of its crust. The Andes of South America, the Alps of Switzerland and Italy, our own Rockies, and the Himalayas of China and Tibet are all young

*The Rocky Mountains in Colorado, which only
formed in the last sixty million years or so*

*The Appalachian Mountains, which are
now old and rounded with age*

mountains that have been thrust up within the past 60 million years or so.

HOW DO MOUNTAINS FORM?

The birth and growth of volcanic mountains are much better understood than the development of mountains that are upthrust and folded out of Earth's crust. One reason is that volcanic mountains are sometimes born overnight and reach a height of several hundred feet in a matter of days or weeks. Scientists can watch the development of these "laboratory" mountains and so come to understand them. But mountains like the Alps and Rockies, which are not volcanic, develop over millions of years and change very slowly.

Many different forces within the planet join to produce mountains—collisions of plates, heat currents in the upper mantle rock, and chemical and physical changes in the materials of the crust and upper mantle, to name a few. Like icebergs, which poke only their heads out of the water, mountains are thought to poke only their heads above the ground. The bulk of their mass—called roots—go deep down into the crustal rock. Because geologists cannot see or collect samples of a mountain's roots, they cannot be sure about them.

Even so, they have an explanation for how a mountain is worn down. We can regard a mountain as a lightweight "rockberg," a rock floating in a sea of heavier fluid rock. Over the centuries the mountain's hard rock is worn away by erosion and washed down onto the surrounding lowland as sediments. All the while, as the mountain loses weight by erosion, the surrounding lowland gains weight by collecting the washed-down materials. The increased weight of sediments pressing down on the lowlands forces some of the fluid material below to move to a region of less pressure—that region being under the mountain, which is becoming lighter by erosion. As more and more fluid rock collects under the mountain's roots, it lifts the mountain. The faster the process of erosion, the faster the mountain rises. This process is called isostasy, which means "equal standing."

The great mountains of the world are made up mostly of sedimentary rocks. Embedded in these sedimentary rocks are fossils of sea creatures that lived long before the mountains rose out of the ancient seas. High in the Alps, for instance, geologists have found the remains of countless forms of sea life.

From time to time in geologic history, great trenches, called geosynclines, have developed in Earth's crust. Age after age, as sediments flowed into the geosyncline, the great ditch slowly sank into the crust. Then something else began to happen. Pressure from the sides of the trench became strong enough to squeeze the sediments deep into Earth and at the same time thrust them up. In the process the thrust-up rock was folded and formed into a wave pattern. The result is a folded mountain chain with deep roots, such as the Appalachians and the Rockies. During the long period of sediment buildup, sea creatures died, drifted to the bottom, and mingled with the layers of sediments to become part of the fossil record. Mountain building by sediment-filled ditches folding upward most likely goes on all the time in one part of the world or another.

CLASSES OF MOUNTAINS

In brief, here is a summary of the basic classes of mountains, based on how mountains are built:

Folded Mountains. The largest mountain systems of the world are folded mountains. They are made up of thick sedimentary rocks that long ago were thrust up by the crust, which squeezed weaker sedimentary materials up into folds. Swit-

THE BIRTH OF FOLDED MOUNTAINS

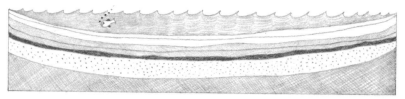

1. Sediments are deposited on the bottom of a shallow sea. As more and more layers accumulate, the weight of those on top compresses those on the bottom into rock.

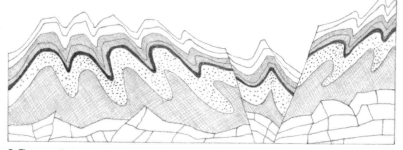

2. The earth below the sea bottom folds and faults, lifting and squeezing the layers of rock into the air to form mountains.

zerland's Jura Mountains and the Appalachians, Rockies, and Sierra Nevadas in North America are all mountains produced by the folding process.

Fault Mountains. Sometimes great breaks occur as faults in Earth's crust. When this happens the ground on one side of the break may slip down hundreds of feet, while the ground on the other side of the break remains as it was. The result is a solid rock wall that may be hundreds of feet high. When the slippage is great enough, a block mountain—also called a fault mountain—is produced. Eventually rain and wind erode the sharp edges of the block, leaving the mountain with a rounded top. Utah, Nevada, and Arizona have several fault mountains of this type.

Volcanic Mountains. As you found earlier, molten rock sometimes flows up through long cracks in the Earth's crust and builds into mountain chains. Also, isolated mountains like Japan's Mount Fuji, Mount Shasta in California, and Mount Hood in Oregon, are the result of volcanic action. Outpourings of lava, cinders, ash, and other materials through a feed pipe pile up over the years and build these lone mountains.

Residual Mountains. Sometimes large, flat areas of land rise up above the surrounding plain rather than fold up into mountains. The result is a plateau. After many years, water draining off the plateau cuts into and eats away the softer earth and rock. At first only shallow ridges of hard rock are left exposed, but over the years these ridges tower higher and higher as the softer parts of the plateau are eaten away. The Allegheny Plateau of Pennsylvania is a region with mountains of the residual type.

CHAPTER NINE

THE OCEANS: SEAFLOOR, CURRENTS, AND CLIMATE

The world's oceans are vast collecting basins for minerals and other materials that are washed away from the continents by rain and carried into the seas by rivers. Meanwhile, the oceans are kept stirred by currents, tides, and waves.

THE RAIN OF SEDIMENTS

The sediments washed into the seas from the land and deposited on the seafloor include sand, gravel, clay, and other matter that today form a muddy carpet averaging some 1,000 feet (300 m) thick. Mixed into the sediment carpet are sharks' teeth, the tiny skeletons of microscopic sea animals, and other materials that form in the seas themselves. This rain of sediment onto the seafloor has been going on for hundreds of millions of years, from the time the continents first formed.

How are the sediments formed? Perhaps you have noticed after a heavy rain that a stream has turned yellow, red, or brown from the soil it has washed from its banks. Many such streams dump their dirty floodwaters into rivers. In turn, the rivers change color as they receive sediment loads from the streams and carry the sediments toward the ocean.

Sometimes these sediments collect at the mouth of a river and form new land, called a delta. For example, the Mississippi delta has increased its size more than four times over the past 150 years.

Sediments are formed by the weathering of rock. The action of water, and of acid rain, chips away or dissolves rock particles. The heating of rock by the Sun and then the cooling by frost cause the rock to expand and contract. As it does, it breaks into tiny pieces. The roots of plants and trees also break ledges and other rock into pieces that eventually become sediments. As glaciers come and go, they bear down on the bedrock beneath the soil as they push their way along. They act as great plows that scrape up the soil and loose rock and grind and scrape their way into the bedrock itself. All this wearing down of the rocks through geologic time is called erosion. So sediments are formed by mechanical action and by chemical and biochemical processes.

The most spectacular example of erosion in the world is the Grand Canyon. Over the past 3 to 4 million years a raging river has carved out the canyon to a depth of 1 mile (1.6 km) and 10 miles (16 km) from edge to edge. The river continues to eat away the rock at a rate of about half a million tons a day.

CONTINENTAL SHELVES AND SLOPES

Many of the sediments washed from the land are carried seaward and settle onto the continental shelves. These are the underwater platform-edges of the continents. They slope gently from a few miles to more than 100 miles (160 km) seaward.

The water covering the continental shelves is not much deeper than about 600 feet (180 m). From time to time great heaps of sediments pile up along the edge of a section of

The Grand Canyon and the Colorado River

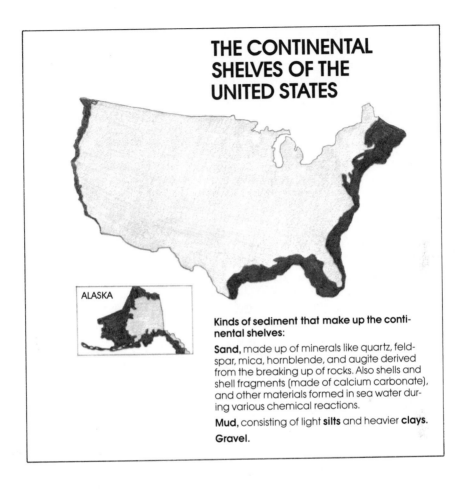

THE CONTINENTAL SHELVES OF THE UNITED STATES

ALASKA

Kinds of sediment that make up the continental shelves:

Sand, made up of minerals like quartz, feldspar, mica, hornblende, and augite derived from the breaking up of rocks. Also shells and shell fragments (made of calcium carbonate), and other materials formed in sea water during various chemical reactions.

Mud, consisting of light **silts** and heavier **clays.**

Gravel.

continental shelf. Then one day a heap may break off and tumble down the continental slope as a rushing sediment slide. Such slides carry some sediments far out onto the deep ocean floor, but most sediments from the land remain near the continental edges.

Those sediments that are carried far out onto the deep ocean floor are very fine grains. They are small particles of red clay about one ten-thousandth of an inch across. Because these particles are so fine it takes years for them to drift down through the 3-mile (5-km) depth of the deep ocean. The red clay carpet of the deep ocean floor collects very slowly—less than 1 inch (2.5 cm) in thousands of years. Added to the red clay are microscopic skeletons of silica and calcium carbonate from tiny animals called plankton that float about near the surface.

ROCK OF THE OCEAN FLOOR

Beneath the thick carpet of seafloor sediments is solid rock. Although it is part of the rock forming the planet's crust, the ocean floor crustal rock is different from the crustal rocks of the continents. Most of the continental rock is granite, but granite is entirely missing in the ocean floor.

The rock beneath the ocean sediments is basalt, that heavy rock that forms from volcanic lava. The granitic rock forming the crust of the continents is about 37 miles (59.2 km) deep. The basaltic rock forming the crust of the ocean floor is only about 6 miles (9.6 km) deep. The bottom of both the continental crust and the ocean-floor crust is not smooth but irregular, like the land surface. Both rest on the thicker and heavier rock layer of the mantle.

MINERALS OF THE OCEANS

Except for certain minor changes, the kinds and amounts of minerals in ocean water have changed little over hundreds of millions of years. Sharks, turtles, and other animals that made the sea their home 300 million years ago would probably be very much at home swimming in the waters of the Gulf of Mexico today.

Minerals are what make ocean water taste salty. Since

ocean water tastes salty, it should not surprise you to learn that the most common mineral in the oceans is salt—sodium chloride. Magnesium, sulfur, calcium, and potassium, in that order, make up the remaining bulk of minerals dissolved in the oceans.

By day the Sun heats the surface waters of the oceans and turns it into water vapor, which is water in the form of a gas. The water vapor rises into the air, cools, and falls back to Earth as rain. The rain feeds the streams and rivers that carry sediments and minerals to the sea, where the cycle begins all over again.

OCEAN CURRENTS AND CLIMATE

The ocean currents follow a general flow pattern that is important in regulating climate. One reason for this is that water can store heat and carry it from one place to another as the currents move. By comparison, the soil is a poor storer of heat. It loses its heat quickly and cannot be heated efficiently to depths of more than a foot or so. Ocean water can be heated to much greater depths. That is why at night the temperature of the ground may become much lower than it is during the day, but the temperature of the surface water of a lake or the ocean changes hardly at all. This ability of water to store heat is what makes winters mild along the coasts compared with harsh temperatures inland.

Like the atmosphere, the oceans are ever in motion. Great rivers of water that we call currents wind their way around the globe, curving this way and that. Currents are very important regulators of climate. Half the heat moved northward and southward from the hot equatorial region is carried by ocean currents. There are many ways in which ocean currents affect climate, but all do so by carrying large amounts of heat or cold from one place to another. In winter,

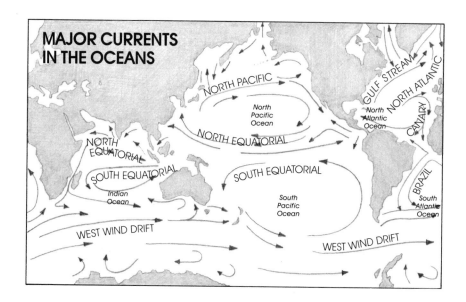

MAJOR CURRENTS IN THE OCEANS

air near the seacoast is generally warmer than air inland. As you found earlier, this is due to the ocean's ability to store heat for longer periods than the land can.

When we trace the course of one of these currents—the Gulf Stream, for example—we can see what important climate regulators the currents can be.

HOW THE GULF STREAM REGULATES CLIMATE

The Gulf Stream begins as a narrow current of warm water flowing out of the Gulf of Mexico off the tip of Florida. The temperature of the surface water there is about 77 degrees F (25 degrees C). Off southern Florida it moves along at a speed of about 90 miles (144 km) a day. The Gulf Stream next swings northeast and up along the U.S. coast at an average speed of about 80 miles (128 km) a day. Off Cape Hatteras, North Carolina, it has cooled a bit to some 72 degrees F (22 degrees C) and begins to branch.

When south of Nova Scotia, the now wider Gulf Stream has slowed to about 45 miles (72 km) a day. Near Newfoundland its northern section mixes with the cold Labrador current flowing down from the Arctic Ocean. As a result of this mixing, the Gulf Stream's water is cooled to about 60 degrees F (15 degrees C). Off the Grand Banks of Newfoundland the northern arm of the Gulf Stream loops around and flows toward western Greenland. Here its warming effect speeds the melting of the sea ice floes brought southward by the East Greenland current. Another arm of the Gulf Stream veers off in a northeast direction and flows to the southwest shores of Iceland. Although cooled to a mere 46 degrees F (8 degrees C), it has a warming effect on Iceland's climate, which otherwise would be much colder.

The main arm of the Gulf Stream flows nearly due east and branches into two before reaching the coast of Europe. The northern arm moves off in a northeasterly direction as a relatively warm current at a speed of about 12 miles (19.2 km) a day. It bathes the shores of Ireland, England, Scotland, and Norway. Oceanographers generally agree that without the Gulf Stream the weather in Europe would be cooler. The harbors of Norway are kept ice-free all year by this warm Atlantic water. But the harbors of Labrador, which are farther south than Norway, do not benefit from Gulf Stream water and are iced over for several months of the year. The northern branch of the Gulf Stream eventually ends in the Arctic Ocean, but not before providing a relatively favorable climate to Spitsbergen, a group of Norwegian islands in the Arctic Ocean.

The southern arm of the Gulf Stream loops down toward the northwest coast of Africa as a current that is cold compared with the surrounding warmer ocean water. Speeded up a bit by winds blowing out of the northeast, this arm of the Gulf Stream joins equatorial water flowing westward and is carried back to Florida again.

Throughout geologic time, climate has been changed by the changing positions of the continents and oceans. For example, millions of years ago large parts of the United States were covered from time to time by shallow inland seas, which made for a warm and moist climate. Such changes, including changes in the temperature of the seawater, undoubtedly have caused certain species of plants and animals to die out. At the same time, certain other species that happened to be well suited for the new climate conditions greatly increased their number. Just such a climate change some 245 million years ago killed off most of the amphibians, who earlier had ruled the land. Cooler and drier conditions favored the reptiles, who replaced the amphibians and dominated the land for a while.

A CURRENT THAT RAN AWAY

Here is an actual example of the many ways a change in a major ocean current can affect living things that depend on that current as a regulator of climate.

In 1925 the cold, northward-flowing Humboldt Current off the coast of Peru, South America, moved seaward and so touched off a chain reaction of events. The shift let warm water from the Equator move down the coast of Peru. The temperature of the coastal water quickly rose by 9 degrees F (5 degrees C).

Most animals living in the oceans are sensitive to a temperature change of even one or two degrees. This sharp rise of 9 degrees turned out to be a killing temperature for the usual rich supply of tiny plant and animal plankton. The temperature rise also killed many small fish. Thus, large numbers of small fish that depended on the plankton for food died either of a lack of food or from too much heat. Larger fish that depended on the smaller fish for food were next to go. Their dead bodies littered the shores for many miles. Thousands of seabirds living on the coast and nearby islands died, since their food supply of the larger fish was also cut off.

But this was not the end link in the chain of events. For years the Peruvians had depended on the bird droppings, called guano, as a highly valued natural fertilizer. As long as there were many birds, the fertilizer supply remained rich. But the change in ocean currents also caused unusually heavy rains, which washed away many tons of guano deposits into the sea. The rains also flooded the neighboring land. They destroyed crops, buildings, roads, and many of the local plant and animal populations. In only a few weeks the current change had brought about dramatic changes on land and sea alike. Although a few months later the Humboldt Current swung back to its earlier position, years passed before Peru recovered.

In our brief lifetime we may witness climate changes that affect our lives in some way or another. Such changes, both small and brief or large and long, have been shaping and reshaping the land and its many life-forms for hundreds of millions of years. Among the largest and longest climate changes are the coming and going of ice ages. Let us now look at what causes these frigid changes in climate.

CHAPTER TEN

GREAT ICE

Scientists who study climate tell us that during more than 90 percent of the past 570 million years the North and South Poles probably were free of ice. Also, during most of that time the average annual world temperature probably was about 72 degrees F (22 degrees C). Palm trees once grew in most areas of what is now the United States. New York State had a climate like the one Florida has today. But ages of ice were to periodically interrupt this semi-tropical setting. There was a glacial period about 500 million years ago, and another that lasted for some 50 million years about 300 million years ago. After that Earth remained free of ice ages for about 250 million years, until the Tertiary period.

THE BIG FREEZE . . .
THEN THE BIG MELT

The Tertiary ushered in a new series of ice ages—times when sheets of ice thousands of feet thick ground their way over vast stretches of the land. During the Tertiary there seems to have been a gradual drop in temperature in the mid-latitudes of the Northern Hemisphere. This is about halfway between the Equator and the North Pole. One possibility for this ancient period of cooling was the gradual movement of the Antarctic continent to its present position at the South Pole. The resulting opening of some seaways and closing of others would have changed the pattern of warm and cold current all around Earth. Winter snows would have gradually built up over the centuries and become packed into ice. Eventually, ice would have covered the entire Antarctic continent—as it does today—to a depth of about 10,000 feet (3,000 m). Antarctica has been buried beneath its thick cap of ice for the past several million years.

Scientists agree that several glacial periods have come and gone over the past few million years. Over the past 700,000 years there have been seven known glacial periods, each separated from the next by a period of warming called an interglacial.

Those of us living in the Northern Hemisphere may now be enjoying the peak of one such warm, interglacial period. According to the climate expert Reid A. Bryson, "To find a time as warm as the past few (thousand) years, we have to go back through a long glacial period to 125,000 years ago." Each cycle of glacial activity—from the peak of one glacial period, through an interglacial period, then to the peak of the next glacial period—lasts about 100,000 years. The warm interval from the end of one glacial period to the beginning of the next lasts about 10,000 years.

The last glacial period reached its peak about 18,000 years ago. It ended about 10,000 years ago. At the peak, ice covered about 30 percent of Earth's total land surface in both the Northern and Southern Hemispheres.

During a glacial period it just snows and snows. But it also rains, although more water than today is deposited on land as snow. Ocean water evaporates and rises into the atmosphere, where it turns to snow and rain. In this way increasing

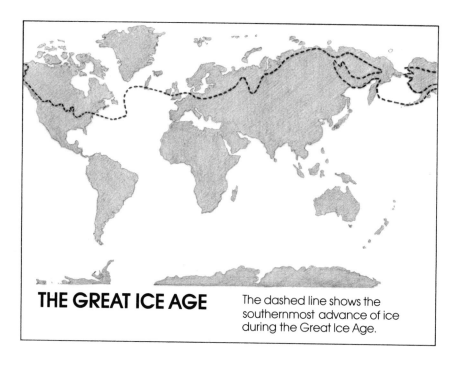

THE GREAT ICE AGE

The dashed line shows the southernmost advance of ice during the Great Ice Age.

amounts of ocean water are evaporated, turned into snow, and dropped on the land, with the result that the sea level lowers quite a bit during an ice age. During the last glacial period the ocean level may have dropped by about 300 feet (90 m). So during a glacial period, large amounts of seawater are locked up as ice.

Although the polar oceans are especially cold and largely ice covered during a glacial period, the ocean water in low latitudes and near the Equator remains warm. During the last ice age of 18,000 years ago, the Caribbean Sea, for example, was a balmy 73 degrees F (23 degrees C) compared with 80 degrees F (27 degrees C) today.

WHY ICE AGES COME AND GO

No one knows for certain what triggers an ice age, but scientists have some ideas. All their theories fall into one of two groups: (1) Ice ages are set off by astronomical events; for example, a decrease in the energy output of the Sun or the Solar System passing through a large cosmic cloud of space dust; and (2) Ice ages are caused by events on the planet itself; for example, changes in the ocean currents or times of widespread mountain building.

The Isthmus of Panama, linking North and South America, was pushed up out of the seafloor about 3.5 million years ago. When this huge land bridge was thrust up it blocked the warm currents flowing westward from the Atlantic into the Pacific Ocean. Thus, an increased amount of warm water was forced into the North Atlantic Ocean toward Newfoundland and Greenland. This larger area of warm water could have led to more evaporation of the ocean water and further could have resulted in increased snow—enough snow to support the growth of ice fields.

Some climatologists think that the northern ice sheets are controlled by the movement of the warm water of the Gulf Stream. According to this theory, the Gulf Stream shifts its position from time to time; it also becomes stronger or weaker. Both changes are thought to cause an alternating spread and retreat of northern ice. In the 1930s, the Yugoslavian scientist N. Milankowitch suggested that Earth's attitude in space in relation to the Sun changes with time and could help cause climate change.

Glacial ice left over from the last ice age still covers much of the land. In its relentless march toward the sea, the ice continues to shape mountain peaks now completely or partly buried beneath the ice. It gouges out enormous valleys and generally carries out earth-moving feats that defy imagination. Today, glacial ice is found on every continent

A glacier-dammed lake in Alaska. Note the icebergs being discharged from the glacier margins.

except Australia and covers about 10 percent of Earth's total land area. The continental glacier that caps Antarctica has enough ice to cover the United States to a depth of 9,000 feet (2,700 m). All this ice is a frigid reminder of those great North American ice sheets of only 10,000 years ago.

The great ice comes and goes. We now seem to be near the end of a global-warming period. After a brief time, geologically speaking, the long-range climate forecast calls for the great ice sheet once again to advance. When it does, it will erase the present and reshape the land anew, as it has done time and again in the past.

THE EARTH IN TIME
Numbers = millions of years ago

MESOZOIC ERA
"Age of Reptiles"

PALEOZOIC ERA
"Ancient Life"

190 M. YEARS AGO

215
PERMIAN TRIASSIC JURASSIC 155 CRETACEOUS 120

590 CAMBRIAN

70 MILLION YEARS AGO

440

235
PENNSYL-
VANIAN ("Age of Amphibians") 265 MISSISSIPPIAN
("Age of Fishes") DEVONIAN 330 SILURIAN 365 ORDO-
VICIAN

PRECAMBRIAN ERA

CENOZOIC ERA
"Recent Life"

PROTEROZOIC

1.8 TERTIARY

QUA-
TERNARY

ARCHAEOZOIC

4.5 billion years ago

GLOSSARY

Accretion. A clumping process of matter that may have caused the planets and their moons to have formed out of the original matter making up the Solar System. That matter probably consisted of ices, rock, and metals, the particles being drawn together, or accreted, by gravity.

Archipelago. A chain of undersea mountains, the tops of which form islands.

Asteroids. Any of millions of rock-metal fragments ranging in size from a fraction of a foot to many yards across and traveling around the Sun in orbits between Mars and Jupiter.

Batholith. A huge mass of igneous rock that formed underground when a large body of magma solidified. In time, erosion and gradual crustal uplift may expose such rock.

Cementation. Certain minerals, such as quartz and calcite, act as a "glue" that "cements" loose sediments, such as gravel and sand, into solid rock. If the sediments are made up of sand, the rock formed is sandstone. If the sediments are gravel, the rock is called conglomerate.

Core. The central region of a star or a planet. Earth's core seems to be a large ball of solid iron and nickel surrounded by a layer of liquid iron and nickel.

Core sample. A hollow tube inserted deep into the ocean floor, for example, can bring up a sample of sediments that can be studied to determine the geologic history of the region.

Crust. The thin layer of rock covering the surface of our planet, reaching about 6 miles (9.6 km) deep beneath the oceans to about 37 miles (59.2 km) deep beneath the continents. Most of the continents are made up of a granite-type rock.

Delta. New land formed by sediments deposited at the mouth of a river.

Dike. A long, wide, but thin body of intrusive igneous rock that cuts across the layering of the surrounding rock formation (see *Intrusion*).

Erosion. The long-term effects of heat, water, wind, ice, and acid rain, which may chip away or chemically dissolve solid rock. The chipped away particles are called sediments. Sediments may be formed by mechanical action or by chemical or biochemical processes.

Extinction. The disappearance of a species or higher group of plants or animals.

Extrusion. Molten rock that has spilled out onto Earth's surface, such as a lava flow.

Fault. A crack or break in Earth's crustal rock. Two surfaces along a fault may strain against each other until the pressure is so great that the two surfaces slip, or snap. The snapping action causes an earthquake.

Focus. The spot where an earthquake occurs, sometimes near the surface and sometimes deep underground. Certain earthquake waves sent out from the focus pass through the planet while others travel around its curved surface.

Geologic time. The portion of time that took place before written history began. It involves a very long span of time, millions and billions of years, much longer than anyone can imagine.

Geosyncline. A great trench that develops in Earth's crust. Over many centuries, as sediments flow into a geosyncline trench, the great ditch, along with its load of sediments, slowly sinks into the crust. Pressure from the sides of the trench squeezes the sediments down and at the same time thrusts them up and folds them. The result may be a folded mountain.

Half-life. The period of time during which one half the number of atoms of a radioactive element change into atoms of a different element. Nothing, including temperature and pressure, appears to affect the half-life of any radioactive element. Different radioactive elements have different half-lives.

Igneous rock. Rock formed when molten material (see *Lava* and *Magma*) flows up from deeper parts of Earth's crust and solidifies either within the crust or at the surface. Of the three kinds of rock described in this book, igneous rock makes up about 65 percent of Earth's crust. Igneous rock may be either intrusive (hidden below Earth's surface) or extrusive (exposed at the surface).

Interglacial. A period of warming between two glacial periods. We may be living in an interglacial period now.

Intrusion. Molten igneous rock that forces its way into surrounding solid rock and solidifies below Earth's surface.

Isostasy. A condition of balance in which a large and high landmass is not supported by solid rock beneath, but by floating in denser but fluid rock of the underlying mantle, similar to an iceberg floating in water.

Laccolith. A mass of igneous rock that formed underground when a body of magma domed up the rock into which it was intruded and solidified. Eventually erosion exposes a laccolith.

Lava. Molten rock (magma) that is forced out of a volcano or out of cracks in Earth's crust and hardens at the surface.

Law of superposition. A principle that states that in the normal layering of sediments, or rock, the more recent layers are found on top of the older layers.

Magma. Fluid rock material originating in the deeper parts of Earth's crust. It is capable of forcing its way up through solid rock. When flowing out over the surface, it is called lava. Lava solidifies into igneous rock.

Mantle. The layer of rock beneath Earth's crust, basically made up of iron and magnesium mixed with silicates. Because the mantle rock is under great pressure from the weight of rock above, the upper mantle is hot and behaves more like putty than a solid. Lower down, the mantle rock is rigid.

Metamorphic rock. Any rock mass of Earth's crust that has been recognizably changed in texture and/or mineral composition by heat or chemically active fluids. Metamorphic rock makes up about 27 percent of Earth's rocks.

Meteorites. Pieces of rock or rock/metal that have survived their journey down through Earth's atmosphere without burning up.

Mineral. Any solid nonliving element or compound found free in nature. Salt and calcite are examples of minerals. The most plentiful minerals are quartz and feldspar, making up about 63 percent of Earth's crustal rock.

Nebula. A great cloud of dust and gas within a galaxy. The nebulae are thought to be the birthplaces of stars and planets.

Nuclear fusion. The union of atomic nuclei and, as a result, the building of the nuclei of more massive atoms. Hydrogen nuclei in the core of the Sun fuse and build up the nuclei of helium atoms. In the process large amounts of energy are emitted, thus accounting for the Sun's energy output.

Oort cloud. A gigantic shell of icy particles mixed with dust enclosing the entire Solar System. Such a shell of matter is believed to be left over from the time the Solar System was formed some 4.6 billion years ago. It also is thought to be the storehouse of comets.

Paleontologist. A scientist who specializes in the recovery and study of fossils.

Pangaea. The single supercontinent that existed about 220 million years ago, when all the landmasses were merged into one. By about 135 million years ago, Pangaea had broken up and drifted apart into a northern half, called Laurasia, and a southern half, called Gondwana.

Planetesimals. Clumps of solid matter that formed out of the solar disk material in the early years of the Solar System. The planetesimals were made up of rock or rock mixed with iron and other metals. Billions of these planetesimals plunged into Earth and the other planets and their moons during the first 700 million years, producing great heat and, later, many craters.

Plate tectonics. A general term for the theory of continental drift. In this theory, now widely accepted as fact, there are six major "plates" forming Earth's crust and about a dozen smaller ones. The continents, along with sections of the ocean floor, are pushed about like giant rafts of stone floating in a sea of molten rock beneath (the mantle).

Radioactivity. A few of the more than 100 known elements "decay" naturally, and in the process change into a different element. As they decay they emit some of the particles (protons) in their nuclei.

Rift valley. A trench, such as the Mid-Atlantic Ridge, along which molten rock from the mantle wells up, flows out onto the surrounding land (or seafloor), hardens, and so forms new crustal rock.

Sedimentary rock. Rock formed from clay, lime, sand, gravel—and sometimes plant and/or animal remains—that have been squeezed under great weight and pressure for long periods of time. Sedimentary rock makes up about 75 percent of the land area of the world. Sedimentary rocks often contain fossils, unlike igneous and metamorphic rocks (see *Cementation*).

Sediments. The loose bits and pieces of clay, mud, sand, gravel, lime, and other earth materials that pile up century after century and become squeezed by the great weight of new sediments above. Eventually, such sediment heaps may be thrust up as new mountains.

Seismic waves. The waves generated when an earthquake snaps a fault. These waves are recorded on instruments called seismographs at seismograph stations around the world. The inked wiggly line recorded by a seismograph during an earthquake is called a seismogram.

Sill. A long, wide, but thin body of intrusive igneous rock that lies parallel to the layering of the surrounding rock formation (see *Intrusion*). The famous Palisades of New Jersey-New York are a sill exposed by erosion.

Weathering. The erosion of rocks and soil by frost and other weather conditions.

INDEX

*Italicized page numbers
indicate illustrations*

Accretion, 12
Archipelago(es), 54–55
Arson, 45
Asteroid(s), 11, 15, *17*
Atmosphere(s), 19–20, 21,
    75, 81
"Atomic clock(s)," 47
Atom(s), 45

Batholith(s), 25, 37
Brongniart, Alexandre, 44
Bryson, Reid A., 81

Cementation, 34
Climate(s)
    change(s) in, 39–40, 50,
      80–85
    effect(s) of ice age(s),
      80–85

    effect(s) of ocean cur-
      rent(s), 75–79, 83
Coal, *39*
Continental drifting of, 50–
    51, 53
    effect(s) on climate, 50
Continental shelves, 71, 73
Continent(s)
    Africa, 52–53
    Antarctica, 39, 52
    Australia, 58, 85
    drifting, 50–51, 53
    Europe, 51
    formation of, 48, 50
    granitic, 50
    India, 53
    N. America, 68, 83, 85
    Pangaea, 48
    S. America, 53, 78, 83
    See also Plate tec-
      tonic(s)
Core sample(s), 40